HENRIK JOHANSEN

VE6C

TROY MODEL CLUB SERIES

OLDER LOCOMOTIVES (1900-42)

OLDER LOCOMOTIVES
(1900-42)

P. G. Gomm

NELSON

THOMAS NELSON AND SONS LIMITED
36 Park Street London W 1
PO Box 27 Lusaka
PO Box 18123 Nairobi
PO Box 21149 Dar es Salaam
77 Coffee Street San Fernando Trinidad
THOMAS NELSON (AUSTRALIA) LIMITED
597 Little Collins Street Melbourne 3000
THOMAS NELSON AND SONS (CANADA) LIMITED
81 Curlew Drive Don Mills Ontario
THOMAS NELSON (NIGERIA) LIMITED
PO Box 336 Apapa Lagos
THOMAS NELSON AND SONS (SOUTH AFRICA) (PROPRIETARY) LIMITED
51 Commissioner Street Johannesburg

First published 1970
SBN 17 213208 8

Photography by Michael Langford

Printed and bound by SIR JOSEPH CAUSTON AND SONS LTD *London and Eastleigh*

CONTENTS

To my family and Rod Flanagan.

'No man is an Island.' I do not think these words were ever more true than in relation to the preparation of this book. I would particularly like to thank Ivor Lindsell, Mrs Chilton, Ian Bew and Mr Willis for the loan of models for photographing, and my thanks for information go to Bob Cutts of St Albans, to Howard T. Moulton of the USA, and to all those who have been kind enough to help.

Full credit for the pictures in this book must go to Michael Langford, with whom it has been a real pleasure to work.

Last but not least, my thanks are due to my family and to my good friend Rod Flanagan. They must have the patience of Job to put up with my near-fanaticism for trains in general and for Hornby trains in particular.

INTRODUCTION

MODEL RAILWAYS IN BRITAIN

Trains seem to have caught the imagination and attention of men and boys ever since the first to carry passengers left the 'Station in Euston Square' for Birmingham on 17 September 1838. This fascination with trains led to a desire to possess, not the real thing, which would be impossible, but the next best thing, namely a replica. At first these replicas or models were professionally built and could be purchased only by the rich. It was not until the beginning of the present century that the hobby of acquiring and operating model railways became a practical possibility for the average man.

The idea of producing model trains in quantity had arisen in the latter part of the nineteenth century, and in this connection the German town of Nuremberg, which was the centre of the European clockmaking industry, was embarking upon an era of importance that it was to enjoy for a good many years. With skilled and cheap labour available, it became the home of such names as Märklin Brothers, Carette, Bub, and Bing Brothers, which were to become synonymous with tin-plate trains.

Before the products of these firms became distributed throughout the world, the models available were predominantly steam-powered, and had only very loose affinities to the trains that were running on the real railways. They were externally fired, which meant that the lamp which heated the water was under the boiler. The cheaper versions were known as 'Piddlers', because of their habit of leaving a watery trail when running! This tendency, and their habit of causing minor fires when they came off the track, made them very unpopular with wives and mothers. With improved methods and other fittings, these faults were later corrected. Made of brass and steel and rarely painted, these models were by today's standard very crude; but their lack of paintwork did have one advantage: they did not show the signs of burning so common in later scale models. At this time, incidentally, there was no standardization on gauges and scales.

In the late Victorian and early Edwardian eras housing conditions and wages were very different from what they are today, and in the pre-1910 period the purchase of reasonable models would have been financially impossible for the majority of people. For example, a Stevens Model Dockyard 4-4-0 and tender named *The Prince* to $2\frac{3}{8}$-inch gauge cost £4 10*s*. 0*d*., and polished mahogany wood carriages cost

13*s*. 6*d*. to 15*s*. 6*d*.; goods rolling stock to the same standard cost 10*s*. 6*d*. and 15*s*. 6*d*. each.

The newly established firm of Bassett-Lowke & Co. was then about to make its mark by issuing a mail order catalogue, which was advertised in one of the first numbers of *The Model Engineer*. This catalogue illustrated the various model engineers' castings, fittings, etc., with pasted-in photographs taken by W. J. Bassett-Lowke, who was an enthusiastic amateur photographer.

In 1900 Bassett-Lowke visited the Paris Exhibition, where he was particularly impressed with the precision limits to which the Continental makers were working. He was so impressed that he arranged for locomotives of his own design to be constructed by Bing Brothers, one of the Continental manufacturers. Stefan Bing, who was Governing Director of the Nuremberg firm, was responsible for a very striking exhibition of household utensils, toy steam engines and clockwork, steam and electrically driven toy railways, and he was very keen to produce model railways of the English types. The result of all this was the design and introduction of a 2½-inch gauge steam-driven model of the London and North-Western Railway's *Black Prince*.

This LNWR model was a practical working reproduction of a particular engine. It was to be the first of a long line of LNWR 4-4-0s in a number of gauges and methods of propulsion. The choice of this type reflects the contemporary railways which were now settling down following the famous 'Races to the North'. The outcome of these races had been an increase in the weight of expresses and therefore the need for larger engines. These locomotives had been built to satisfy that need, and they were new. Model engines have always tended to copy the new passenger trains rather than goods. Engines with six driving wheels were being used for the latter, but they were not modelled generally until later.

Shortly after this, Henry Greenly, who was to be responsible for so many estate railways, and for the famous locomotives of the Romney, Hythe and Dymchurch Railway and the Ravenglass and Eskdale Railway, joined the firm as Consultant Designer. The immediate result was the first commercially produced scale model locomotive built from castings—a 3¼-inch gauge model of a Midland Railway 4-4-0—and also a clockwork 'O' gauge saddle tank locomotive. This latter model, fitted with reversing gear, was, with the *Black Prince*, a standard product until 1914.

It was now necessary to define a series of standard scales and gauges, and this Henry Greenly did, basing them on Continental measurements. This meant that products to these new standards were inter-changeable, and, with the vastly improved production methods, the hobby of model trains really began to grow. Gauges 3 and 2 were then quite common, while gauge 1 dominated the play-rooms.

In 1910 a shop was opened by Bassett-Lowke at 112 High Holborn, which was to become probably the most famous model railway shop in the world. Bassett-Lowke had opened their first shop, at 257 High Holborn in 1908, but they moved to No. 112 when business demanded larger premises. Here, and at Gamages, also in High Holborn, one could see and buy the best of the types available. Gamages had their own stamp on some of these trains, and they are now much sought-after by collectors.

In that year, 1910, Bassett-Lowke produced 30,000 models of a Cardean 4-6-0, together with passenger coaches in 'O' gauge clockwork, for the Caledonian Railway in Scotland; they could be bought at the Railway Company's bookstalls at 2*s.* 6*d.* for the locomotive, and 1*s.* 6*d.* for the coaches.

In 1914 the outbreak of war immediately put a stop to the supply of Continental models, and the Bassett-Lowke works went over to work for the Ministry of Munitions. In another part of the country, experiments had begun, and were continuing, with a new part of a construction system. From these rather odd beginnings, a series of model trains were developed which were to become a household name the world over. The constructional system was Meccano, and the idea was to market a constructional locomotive having a specially designed clockwork motor. During the war it had to be shelved, and for some time after the Armistice in 1918 the factory was occupied in making up for lost time in the production of Meccano; but the possibility of clockwork trains was not forgotten, and experiments were put in hand to develop the earlier ideas. In 1920 it was decided to commence the manufacture of clockwork trains, and in that year the first 'Hornby Train' was placed on the market. These trains, which were 'O' gauge, were unique in that they were built up from standard parts and could be taken to pieces and rebuilt.

These first locomotives were a freelance 0-4-0 in the colours of London and North Western, Great Northern, Caledonian, and London, Brighton and South Coast railway systems. They are very difficult to recognize unless one is familiar with the liveries of these railways, as there are no Company markings. The only marks other than the trade mark, which was then M.Ltd.L. (standing for Meccano Ltd, Liverpool) was number 2710 on the locomotive. (It is interesting to note that this was one of Meccano's Liverpool telephone numbers.)

In the early 1920s imports of Continental manufactured items began to come back, but with stiffer competition from their English competitors. Hornby were covering the lower end of the price range in the small scales with their 0-4-0, but Bassett-Lowke, back again with their Continental manufactured items, were beginning to receive competition at the scale end. For instance, the Leeds Model Co. started a range of ready-to-run locos in 1921, with a 4-4-0 in the North Eastern, Midland, and the London and North Western Railways' liveries.

The years after the war also saw a continuation of the reduction in scales and gauges. This was to some extent due to external circumstances, but, within the hobby, experience and the continuing improvements in manufacturing standards meant that the smaller models were equal to or even better than the larger forerunners.

In keeping with this, Bassett-Lowke made an excursion into the '00' gauge field between 1924 and 1926. Made for them by Bing, this gauge was available with quite a wide range of track and accessories. Propulsion was by clockwork or 6 Volt electric with batteries, but, because of a general lack of interest, and also as a result of the Depression, it was dropped in 1926. The general manufacture of the most popular 'O' and '1' gauges continued, but the range did not expand as it might have done in a better financial climate. The main change was in the adoption of the new liveries of the 1923 amalgamation of the railways into the LMS, the LNER, GWR and Southern Systems.

This made life a lot easier for the manufacturers, because they now had only four main companies to follow instead of the previous many. For instance, the LNW, the Midland and the Caledonian Railways were the main constituents of the LMS, and the LNWR 4-4-0, which was being produced in model form in such large numbers, was now issued in red instead of black.

The year 1927 saw the introduction of the Bassett-Lowke *Duke of York*. This was destined to be their most popular model, and about 100,000 were produced. The year of manufacture was used as the number. Hornby used the same numbering scheme with some of their M Series, for instance 2526, 2930 and 3435.

At the turn of the century the real railways had a variety of different liveries and designs. Most of the Companies were then using 'Singles' engines, which meant that they had just two driving wheels. By 1910 four driving wheels was becoming universal; hence the predominance of these in the early products from the model manufacturers. In the late 1920s, and all through the 1930s, the accent was on speed and comfort, and, to provide this, larger locomotives with six driving wheels, and with streamlining, were being built, and in due course these were produced in model form. The range of available items multiplied, and the 'glamour' engines of the main railways, such as the *Flying Scotsman*, the *Royal Scot* and the *Silver Link*, were invading the model layouts.

Bassett-Lowke had not been deterred by their previous experience with the 'OO' gauge models, and in 1935 they offered the Trix Twin Trains which were to be available in unaltered form, but with additions, until well into the late 1950s. This model was electric from the beginning, and by arrangement of the pickups it was possible to operate two trains on the same track. Not to be outdone, other manufacturers began to offer 'OO' gauge models, and in 1938 Hornby offered their new Hornby Dublo. It was to prove ahead of its time technically (an advantage it was to lose after World War II), being available in 12 Volt DC and in clockwork. These were probably the best models available in large quantities in this period prior to the war.

METHODS OF OPERATION

The propulsion of the steam engines in these smaller gauges was by means of methylated spirit, with burners outside the boiler. Clockwork was used by most indoor operators, and these clockwork engines were generally available up to '2' gauge.

Electric operation did not get going until the 1920s and did not really settle down until after World War II. Early models could be anything from 4 Volts, from accumulators or batteries, to, believe it or not, mains 200–250 Volts AC—which were controlled by means of a regulator and a bulb in series to make their operation less dangerous. Needless to say, this method had a very short life. The more usual models were battery operated, at 4, 14, or 20 Volts AC, or 6, 8, or 12 Volts DC.

Reverse operation of some of the AC models was by means of automatic reversers, which were operated by cutting the current off and then applying full power. The only trouble with this system was that dirt on the track could bring the reverse into operation in normal running—with hair-raising results!

World War II put an end to production of toy trains, just when many new developments were under way, and when production began again the picture was very different, but that is another story.

MODEL RAILWAYS IN THE USA

There has never been a great deal of traffic in model railway components across the Atlantic, largely because of a lack of intimacy with the prototypes in each case. Some American manufacturers, such as Ives and Lionel, managed a fair trade; the latter even manufactured some types specially to English Standards.

At the turn of the century, the American model trains were mostly either clockwork or steam-powered, some of the latter being imported from England; but, as we shall see later, battery-operated electric locomotives were available.

Connecticut was the clock centre of the United States, and it was from here that the use of clockwork for model trains had spread. During the latter half of the nineteenth century refinements on some of these early clockwork models included whistles, and even cigarette smoking devices, to try to add realism. The increasing use of clockwork and, later, electric power caused an almost total eclipse of steam power for model trains in the early years of the century. An attempted revival of the use of steam in the 1930s, which included the use of electrically heated boilers, did not succeed.

Electric trains appear to have come on to the American model market in the 1880s and 1890s, and by 1900 there was quite a range available in a number of gauges. One manufacturer, Carlisle and Finch, offered four sizes of steam-type locomotives, a mining locomotive and its rolling stock, and even trolley cars (tramcars). Unfortunately, World War I brought a permanent end to production for this company.

One of the first new names in model railways in the twentieth century became one of the most famous. Lionel's first trains were $2\frac{7}{8}$-inch gauge two-rail electric. Later, in 1903, they introduced steam outline trains and trolley cars in standard $2\frac{1}{8}$-inch gauge, a gauge they were to use until 1939, longer than any other manufacturer. Later additions were electric outline locos in 1910, 'O' gauge three-rail trains in 1915, 'O' gauge clockwork from 1933 to 1937, and 'OO' gauge two- and three-rail from 1938.

Other names which became known at about the same time as Lionel were Howard Knapp and Voltamp, who both manufactured 2-inch gauge two-rail electric models. Voltamp were the largest of these, and they sold out in 1923 to Boucher, who then produced standard gauge three-rail models, but for only one more year.

Ives was one of the oldest names in American model trains, having started in Connecticut in the 1870s. In 1900 they produced only trackless models, but in 1901 they became the first company in the United States to make 'O' gauge clockwork track trains, and they followed these with '1' gauge in 1904; only Ives and Electoy ever used this gauge. They had another first in 1910, when they issued three-rail 'O' gauge electric trains; and they produced '1' gauge in 1912. In 1921 '1' gauge was dropped in favour of Standard gauge. In 1928 bankruptcy overtook the company; due mainly to an over-generous company/customer policy. Control of the company was taken over by American Flyer and Lionel, and items from these companies appeared with Ives nameplates. Lionel used the Ives name exclusively with its own from 1931 to 1933, when it was faded out. During the early part of the century, two former employees of Ives had copied Ives' products and issued them under the American Miniature Railway Co. label.

American Flyer had its beginnings in 1907, when Edmunds Metzel of Chicago, who traded in hardware, produced clockwork trains for Haffner. The success of these led to the formation of the American Flyer Manufacturing Company. Developments during this company's lifetime included three-rail 'O' gauge in 1918, standard gauge (known by Flyer as 'wide gauge') from 1925 to 1936; clockwork models were discontinued in 1937. Gilbert, the Erector manufacturers, bought this company out in 1938 and continued to produce 'O' gauge, but they also produced 3/16-inch scale, and two-rail HO, equipment in 1938.

Haffner produced 'O' gauge tin-plate clockwork trains from 1914 to 1951, and in the 1930s they and Marx were probably the largest producers of clockwork locomotives.

Dorfan manufactured three-rail 'O' gauge trains from 1924, and standard gauge from 1926, until all production finished in 1936. They made the only standard gauge lithographed freight vehicles ever produced in the United States.

For sheer size in 'toy' trains of the 1920s and 1930s the Buddy 'L' line of 'push-alongs' would take some beating. Consisting of a steam loco and nearly a dozen different freight cars (goods wagons) on $3\frac{1}{4}$-inch gauge track, and a smaller one on 2-inch gauge, they were made of sheet steel and were quite realistic.

As in Europe, the early source of electric power was by batteries, but, from World War I onwards, increasing use was made of transformers to supply any voltage from 6 to 25, AC, as required.

Most of the companies referred to made accessories for their trains, even down to quite small items in some cases.

STARTING A COLLECTION

It will be realized that this review must necessarily be incomplete. To cover the ground completely would require many volumes; indeed the activity of almost any one of the companies mentioned would fill a book.

The following plates illustrate some of the items available from the many manufacturers during the period 1900 to 1942. We must apologize if not all of them are in showroom condition, but most of them are at least thirty years old, and are toys which have been 'well used'.

If you are thinking of starting a collection of model trains, there are one or two points worth remembering. First, decide exactly what you are going to collect; secondly, decide what you can afford by having a look at the prices being asked, and then decide what you can store, remembering that trains take up a good deal of space. 'o' gauge takes up four times the space that is required for 'oo' gauge, and larger gauges proportionately more. Specialize in one type or make, bearing in mind that a small but complete collection is more interesting than a large one with no theme.

There are a number of ways of acquiring items for your collection. The easiest way is through dealers, but this is also the most expensive, except on the rare occasions when you come across a bargain, which is still possible even in the West End of London. The other way is to take pot luck with local purchases. Here you can advertise for items in your local paper, or in some other way that you may think of—even, for example, with a 'Wanted' card in any local shop that will co-operate. You may also be able to add to your collection by visiting Jumble Sales and local auctions.

The main thing is to let as many people as possible know what you want, so that they can look for you as well. If you are interested in Hornby 'O' gauge trains, then you may wish to know about the Hornby Railway Collectors Association. Details will be provided with pleasure if you send a stamped addressed envelope to 71, Foster Hill Road, Bedford, England.

The collector's most important attribute is patience, because you never know when, or whence, that wagon you thought impossible to acquire may come.

THE MODELS

SOUTHERN

1 'PIDDLER' AND MÄRKLIN

From the beginning of this century we have a 'before' and early 'after'. The lower picture shows a late nineteenth-century 'Piddler', produced by Stevens Model Dockyard. There are only two real similarities with any form of prototype: it is steam-driven and it runs on rails. The example shown here is steamed regularly and is therefore in its normal condition. It has only about enough power to move itself, although it has not been tested with a load. The spirit holder is under the rear of the engine and from here a tube runs forward; the end of the tube is under the right-hand buffer. Upwards from this tube are the wick holders. The wicks are soaked with methylated spirit, and when they are lit the flames heat the underside of the boiler, which has been filled with water. At the back end of the boiler is a glass tube showing the water level. Thus primed, the engine can be put on the track and left to heat up. The steam from the boiling water is fed to the pistons through the pipes from the top of the boiler. The pistons are of the oscillating type, which means that they pivot (another source of leakage) and are connected to the larger centre driving wheels. Once there is a good head of steam, a spin of the wheels will set the model in motion.

For running on the track shown here the wheels could be set at angles to ease friction. The engine is supplied with an all-curved track; without this and the fact that the track is cambered it would almost certainly fly off the rails, and would be difficult to retrieve because the model gets very hot.

On the front is a tap which can only be for draining the boiler. The chimney is a loose fitting, and serves no useful purpose. Next is the dome, and behind this is the safety valve. Lastly, the whistle, which if used causes a serious loss of power, can also act as a regulator, although to try to stop the locomotive once it is moving is liable to end in blistered fingers. The spectacle plate on the rear end of the boiler is typical of the amount of protection that was provided on the real railways at this time.

The 'Piddler' is to 3¼-inch gauge, and an impression of its size can be got from its comparison with the Märklin 0-4-0 shown above it. This is typical of the smaller Nuremberg products, which tended to have no prototypes; they were simply generalized models of the railway engines of their time. This model, although made for the English market, has German-style numbering, and, like all the other models illustrated, except those in plate 12, it is 'O' (1¼-inch) gauge.

5600
G N R
1442

2 BING FOR BASSETT-LOWKE

After W. J. Bassett-Lowke visited the Paris Exhibition in 1900 he started a long association between these two firms. Their future from then on in England is so interwoven that it is very difficult to separate just four models of each to illustrate. Those shown here were made in Nuremberg and supplied to Bassett-Lowke in the early 1920s.

Top picture: The red 4-6-0 is a model of the LNWR *Prince of Wales* after it had been absorbed into the LMS at the amalgamation of 1923. The class had been initiated in 1911 to work the North of England and Scottish expresses from Euston. Originally they were painted black, but after 1923 the LMS decided to use the Midland Railway style, which is illustrated here. This locomotive was withdrawn from service in 1933, and for the last six years of its life it had a tender different from the type shown.

Second picture: The green 4-4-2 Atlantic locomotive is from the Great Northern Railway. The design was the outcome of famous railway races, after which trains were much heavier than those which had been handled by the single driving wheel types. They were acquired by the LNER in 1923, and one such is shown in Plate 6. The model illustrated here makes an interesting comparison. The number carried by this model is that of the Royal engine, which means that it was always considered first for hauling the Royal train when this was used. It was also displayed at the White City Exhibition in 1909, next to the type it replaced. It was finally scrapped in 1947.

Third and Fourth pictures: The final pair of locomotives are the Bing shortened versions of their *Precursor* 4-4-2 tank engine, which were produced in a number of gauges. This shortened version was produced to enable better operation on layouts with sharp curves. The lower of the two is depicted as it was originally issued in LNWR livery, while the red locomotive is in the early LMS colours. The numbers bear no relation to any prototypes: on the upper engine is that of an 0-6-0 tender engine; the lower number is that of an 0-6-0 Special tank engine.

513

3 GAMAGES

For many years the great attraction at this store in London's High Holborn was the annual Christmas model railway, and the catalogue that was issued annually to mark this occasion was a 'must' for all boys. All the items shown on the facing plate were purchased through the store, and carry the now sought-after Gamages' stamp.

The 'bo-bo' electric locomotive (so called because it had two four-wheeled driving bogies) in the bottom right-hand corner is a Märklin product. It was based on the locomotives introduced on the Paris to Orléans railway prior to World War I. As can be seen, the body is to a bigger scale than 'O' gauge and it would appear to have the same body as the '1' gauge version also produced. The large lights at each end are typical of these Märklin engines.

The train next to this is a Bing set produced for Gamages. Known as *Apollo*, the locomotive is a standard Bing 0-4-0 in LMS colours. The large bulb fitted to the front of the engine appears later to have been copied by Hornby for their own electric trains. In the official catalogue description of this engine it was stated that it was produced to meet the demand for a cheaper type with a good mechanism as fitted to the *George the Fifth* (see plate 5). The outline has some pretensions to scale, and, as it is only a four-coupled engine, the absence of friction allows it considerable hauling capacity. My experience with these 0-4-0s confirms that they are excellent runners. There is no connection with the real LMS 513, which was an ex-Midland Railway 4-4-0. Ex-LNWR 513, on which the design was based, was named *Precursor* and was given the number 5278 by the LMS; the engine named *Apollo* was LNWR 1115, and later LMS 5205. They were all 4-4-0s. The four-wheeled coaches with opening doors are standard Bing.

The other locomotive on this page was made by Märklin. It is much nearer to its LMS counterpart than our previous subject. It is a model of ex-Midland Railway 999s which were 4-4-0s operating the Scottish express service over the famous Settle and Carlisle line.

The coaches and goods rolling stock shown in the corner are Märklin, and, as you can see, include Continental-style wagons with English markings and are companions to the 0-4-0 shown in the first picture.

1269
L B & S C R
11
L N E R
4390
SOUTHERN
773

4 BING PRODUCTS

Although Bing manufactured for Bassett-Lowke, not all the range entered England through them. Some items appeared in both catalogues, and some came via other agents.

Top picture: This is an LNWR 'cauliflower' 0-6-0. Just why the German firm should produce so many LNWR models is not clear. Perhaps the Premier Line's publicity got through to Nuremberg. That shown is one of the few models to have a six-wheeled mechanism before World War I. Although not an accurate representation, it has all the characteristics of the 'cauliflower', the standard LNWR goods engine of the time. The number is correct for the type and it later became LMS 8319. There was also a Great Northern version of the model and both had been discontinued by the 1920s.

Second picture: Its twin is probably better known to railway enthusiasts in its LNWR colours as a *Precursor* tank engine, a variation of the 4-4-0 tender engines. A shortened version is illustrated in plate 2. The LB & SCR Number 11 was a I2 4-4-2 tank engine and would be seen on local services on that system.

Third picture: The LNER 4-4-0 was a model introduced in the 1920s to fill the gap in the Bing range between the LNWR 4-4-0 shown in the next plate and the later *Duke of York*. The bodies of both the clockwork and the electric versions were the same, and that shown is the electric one. The real 4390 was a class D2 4-4-0 and later became No. 2186. The class could be found on lighter trains on the former Great Northern lines.

Fourth picture: The 4-6-0 is another one of those items where one model served several purposes. It was available as shown as Southern Railway's *King Arthur*, as LMS' *Royal Scot*, as LNER's *Flying Fox* and as GWR's *Windsor Castle*. All these were at that time the latest crack express engines of each railway. The one shown has the wrong number for the Southern Railway's *King Arthur*. The correct number was 453, which is for some unknown reason carried on the 0-4-4 tank engine shown in plate 11. The real locomotive with number 773 was in the King Arthur class and was named *Sir Lavaine*. Why all these wrong numberings should occur is a mystery, unless it was because there were not the number of railway books available then. The other models in this series carried the correct details. The odd man out, because it was in fact a 4-6-2, was the LNER *Flying Fox*. The *Windsor Castle* was for obvious reasons the Great Western Royal engine.

5320
GREAT
WESTERN

5 GEORGE THE FIFTHS (BING)

I have given these a whole page to themselves to illustrate a few of their large number. It will immediately be obvious that the first, third and fourth locomotives are the same except for the livery carried. As with the last on the previous page, this is another example of one model serving a multitude of purposes.

Top picture: This is the original of the species and it correctly depicts number 2663 *George the Fifth* of the LNWR, the leader of the class of the same name. These were built by Bing in at least 'O', '1', and '11' gauges, and were powered by clockwork and electricity. The LNWR and LMS versions bore a very fair resemblance to the prototype, but in all the other liveries they are completely inaccurate, although even the Great Western livery did seem to suit them.

Second picture: This is the odd one out in that it is the *de-luxe* version of the above. As will be seen, it is basically the same with detail differences. The front bogie, for example, is much more correct in length and in the size of wheels, and the driving wheels are finer with better connecting rods. These modifications give it better proportion than the others, which appear to have their bogies too far forward. Other detail added to the body include lamp irons, a more accurate dome, wheel splashers and vacuum pipes. Better detail on the tender include axle boxes which are proper bearings. Number 2664 *Queen Mary* was built at Crewe in 1910 as a saturated type, and it was the leader of a class of that name. In 1913 and 1914 this small class, which then totalled six, were converted to superheated types and became *George the Fifths*.

Third picture: This *George the Fifth* is shown in the early LMS livery, which is correct except that it did not have the crest on the cabside but just had the initials there.

Fourth picture: Finally, in this selection, is the Great Western type. The only connection between this model and any real Great Western engine is the fact they are both 4-4-0s. Again we have an example of the wrong number-and-name combination. The number shown here is that of the *City of Bath,* of which we shall see a better model later, whereas the name is from a *Duke* class engine No. 3287.

L B & S C R
22
STEPHENSON
329
L N E R

6 MÄRKLIN

The products of this famous firm were first distributed in England at the beginning of the century. The range over the years consisted of German, French and English types available in clockwork, electric and steam in 'O' and '1' gauges. Some of the more interesting items they produced included a Centenary Train for their local Nuremberg line and the diesel *Flying Hamburger* streamlined train. One of the few firms to have lasted in its original form, they manufactured 'O' gauge models up to the early 1950s. They joined the 'OO' field in the late 1930s using 20 Volts AC.

All the locomotives illustrated here are from the 1920s and are typically very high and look heavy. The knob next to the dome on each one is the speed control.

Top picture: The 4-4-2 tank engine carries the livery of LB & SCR number 22. The London, Brighton and South Coast Railway was a system covering the area of its name, and in 1923 it became part of the Southern Railway. Number 22 became a member of the I3 class which were used for light local services radiating from Brighton, including the service now covered by the Bluebell Railway.

Second picture: The 4-6-4 tank is another 'Brighton' engine, this time of the *Remembrance* class. This class was started in 1919, with the first locomotive being given the name 'Remembrance' in memory of the LB & SCR workers who lost their lives in World War I. They were built to work the fast trains between London and Brighton, a journey which, although not long in distance, had to be covered as quickly as possible. Later in the 1930s they were converted to 4-6-0 tender engines and classified as N15Xs, with the painted names transferred to plates.

Third picture: This is a clockwork *Ivatt Atlantic,* the name given to the 4-4-2 wheel arrangement, in LNER colours. This model is based on the locomotives working expresses on the main line from King's Cross.

7 IVES AND LIONEL

As we have said in the Introduction, there has never been any real two-way traffic in model locomotives across the Atlantic. The prototype railways were so vastly different, and obviously sales of model trains have tended to reflect the local scene. Of the American manufacturers, Lionel are probably the best known in Europe, and this page consists of their direct or indirect products.

Ives did send quite a lot of their production over to England in the early 1930s, and the electric locomotive in the bottom right-hand corner is probably one of these. In this colour, and carrying the number 1651, it was made about 1932–3. Although it bears the Ives name, this locomotive, with its matching coaches on the left, was in fact made by Lionel at their New Jersey factory, and it has their latch couplings and mechanism. They were called transitional trains and were described as being of New York, New Haven and Hartford box electric type. The New York, New Haven and Hartford Railroad had opened electrified sections of its line in 1894. The coaches bear all the signs of production by Lionel; they carry the numbers 1691 on the car with verandah, and 1690 on each of the others.

The steam train heading through the middle is from an Ives series issued about 1916. The locomotive is No. 19, and it usually came with the No. 17 tender as shown here. The engine body is cast iron and to English eyes rather ugly but somehow charming. The tender and coaches are all made of tin-plate. The coaches are, in order: Parlour Car No. 62, Chair Car No. 61 and Baggage Car No. 60 with opening doors.

The engine in the top left-hand corner is a Lionel 259E, which was in production from 1933 to 1938. The E in the number means that it contains a three-stage mechanical, remote control reverse mechanism.

L M S
6285
L M S
13000

8 LIVE STEAM

On this plate are a selection of steam models from the 1930s. By this time steam-driven models had gone from the general scene, and the three locomotives shown are just about all that were available.

Top picture: This 2-6-0 started a very long run in 1937, and it is the only model in this book which is still in production today. Originally it cost 5 guineas and is now over 100 guineas: probably the most accurate 'O' gauge steam model produced in large quantities, it was based on the LMS Stanier 2-6-0. The various parts do not serve the same purpose on the model that they did on the real engine. For instance, the dome hides the combined boiler filler and safety valve, and the smoke box at the front end comes away to reveal the lubricator. This locomotive was available in the liveries of all four railways, but the only model that could be accurate to the type was the LMS, and in consequence it outnumbered the others in production figures by about two to one.

Second picture: This model is probably equally famous to older enthusiasts. It is, of course, the Bassett-Lowke *Enterprise* of the early 1930s, when it cost 45*s*. The signs of use are obvious and are quite common on these models. In the late 1930s the *Super Enterprise* became available at 63*s*, and was a 4-6-0. The model illustrated here is the LNER version, and it carries the number of an O4 class 2-8-0, which later became 3739.

Third picture: This is a Bowman 4-4-0. This Luton-based firm made a range of steam toys which included other engines, all 0-4-0 tanks. Cheapest of all those shown, it cost 35*s* when issued in the early 1930s. Non-reversing, with oscillating cylinders, they were the modern 'Piddlers'. The model shown here has the number and livery of an LMS *Crab* 2-6-0. Numbers given to these models were many and varied, and they seem to have been chosen for topicality. Examples of LNER versions include 234 *Yorkshire,* which was a 4-4-0, and 4472 *Flying Scotsman,* which is, of course, a 4-6-2.

7118
6
C R
77
GREAT WESTERN

9 BONDS, L.M.C. AND WALKER FENN

The locomotives shown in this plate represent semi-scale running or appearance.

Top picture: On the left is an LMS ex-Midland Railway 3F tank engine. Made by Bonds of Euston Road, London, it is a very good representation of the real 7118. It was one of the famous 'Jinties' or 'Jockos' which were to be found all over the LMS system, as shunters in yards and stations or working on branch lines. Sometimes the same engine spent years at one place and even acquired a local nickname. One of these models achieved fame by pulling a man at the Model Railway Club exhibition in the Kingsway Hall in 1927. On the right is another of the small shunter family. This was not one of the main railway companies' types but was based on the products of the famous Pecket works. They were used mainly on industrial railways such as those serving mines, large factories and docks. Again they rarely strayed, and more often than not were painted in the elaborate livery of the owning company. Known universally, the bonzone had a few changes over the years. When first released in the 1920s it had a flat back, whereas that illustrated is from the 1930s. The centre wheels were on stub axles, and it was later possible to run it with flanges on all wheels, which would help adhesion. The mechanism was the standard Märklin four-coupled type, and the body was available in black, green, or yellow. The lid to the tool box is in the open position to show the winding spindle.

Second picture: The Caledonian Railway No. 77 is a Pickersgill 4-4-0 built for that railway at the end of World War I. Built to take the Scottish expresses North of Carlisle, they put up some very good performances. The model is by the Leeds Model Co. and was available in the 1920s. It also appeared in the Bassett-Lowke catalogue.

Third picture: The third pair of 0-6-0 tank engines are by Märklin and Walker Fenn. They were, in fact, standard Märklin products fitted with a speed control on the clockwork mechanism developed by Walker Fenn. The model on the left shows signs of a favourite Märklin habit, in that the new livery has been painted over the original. They also treated other rolling stock in this way.

Fourth picture: This is another LMC model, this time of a Great Western *Castle* class 4-6-0. This was one of their special models, and it is a very good example of the pre-war standards of small-scale modelling. A number of firms offered this special model service.

M R
LNWR
G
FAIR MAID
LNER
5671
GREAT WESTERN

10 CARETTE, EXLEY AND WINDSOR

This page is rather a mixture with no real theme except that it shows the products of some smaller manufacturers. Carette was a Frenchman who moved to join the Germans at Nuremberg and who developed a thriving toy-making business. Both Exley and Windsor were English companies, the former being still in business making rolling stock.

Top picture: The row of wagons are from Carette and have his distinct coupling, but otherwise they are very similar to those from the other Nuremberg makers. They are from the 1920s, and carry the liveries of some of the pre-1923 grouping railways.

Second picture: The steam railcar is a model by Exley of a vehicle made by Sentinels for the LNER. A number of these were produced for use on local services. *Nettle,* which was another LNER railcar of the same design, was produced by the Leeds Model Company. More common than the Exley, it had lithographed paper sides, was powered by a Leeds motor bogie, and was, of course, cheaper. Running as a trailer to the *Fair Maid* is a four-wheeled LSWR coach by the Windsor Model Company.

Third picture: This more obvious steam railcar represents an earlier attempt at making a self-contained branch-line unit. In the early years of this century the railways were beginning to feel the effects of the competition from road transport, especially the tramcar. To compete with this, and to make for easier operation, the railways decided to try these combined units. They could be driven from either end, which saved time and trouble, but on the debit side they were not available at all if the locomotive needed servicing, and it could not operate any freight trains. The example shown here is in South Eastern and Chatham Railway livery and was made by Carette. It is steam driven with a vertical piston in the driver's cab.

Fourth picture: This is a Windsor Model Company model of Great Western 5671, which was one of their standard 0-6-2 tank engines. The Windsor Model Company is probably the least-known manufacturer in this whole series, but they had the laudable policy of building the best model possible at a reasonable price. They were also brave enough to make a model of an LMS Beyer-Garratt 2-6-0-0-6-2 articulated locomotive. This was made for use with twin clockwork motors, which were synchronized for direction through a system of levers.

SOUTHERN
453
MODEL
RAILWAY ENGINEERS
R.F. STEDMAN & Co. Ltd.
HUNSLET, LEEDS
36
BRENTNALL & CLELAND
B & C
684
LONDON
LOAD 12 TONS
G W
CARDIFF
17954
25 Tons
6362
GREAT WESTERN

11 THE LEEDS MODEL COMPANY

The Leeds Model Company began production in 1921, and they produced a wide range of model railway equipment until the company's demise a few years ago. One of the directors in the early years was R. F. Stedman, who also made some equipment under his own name. In the 1930s he left the company to manufacture under his own name and to try other activities, but he returned to model railways after the War.

Top picture: The 0-4-4 tank engine is another case of the standard locomotive style serving a number of purposes. It is a Stedman product, and for some reason best known to Mr Stedman, it again carries the number of an entirely different type of locomotive. Its number, 453, was the number of the Southern Railway express 4-6-0 *King Arthur*. The open coal wagon is our first example of a manufacturer making a model wagon with his own name on it. As we shall see, Bassett-Lowke and Hornby also used the idea.

Second picture: These are two models of goods rolling stock from LMC. Again an open coal wagon, but this time bearing the name of an actual coal merchant. From 1845 to the 1940s examples of these could be found practically anywhere in the British Isles. They were owned by individual merchants, each of whom might have had any number of wagons, from just a single one to a large fleet. The railways contracted to take the wagons backwards and forwards from the merchant's yard or siding to the colliery. The Great Western brake, or guard's van, is in the same series, and it represents the type in use on that railway. As usual, it was also available in the other railway designs, and there were *de-luxe* versions with more detail.

Third picture: This is an R. F. Stedman Great Western model. Typically, it is not an absolute scale model, but it has all the character of the prototype. These were general-purpose engines of the GWR and, as such, they could be seen on all sorts of trains.

Fourth picture: Finally, there is an LMC Midland Railway full parcels brake coach. As their name implies, these vehicles were used to carry mail and newspapers either in parcels trains or at the end of a passenger train. Made by LMC in the 1920s, it has a wooden box body with paper lithographed sides.

L N E R
4498
NE
270341
L M S
BASSETT-LOWKE Ltd
L M S
SHELL
LUBRICATING
OIL
ESSO
L M S
L M S
L N E R
L M S
3302
LMS
LMS

12 'OO' GAUGE TRAINS

All the 'OO' gauge trains have been put on one page to illustrate just how limited this gauge was compared with the present time, when it is the most popular gauge. Even in the 1940s a lot of modellers were saying that it would not become popular, in much the same way that it has been said that 'N' gauge will not.

At the top of the page there is the Hornby Dublo LNER A4 *Sir Nigel Gresley*. Introduced in 1937, and available in clockwork or 12 Volt DC electric, it will be obvious that it was far ahead of anything else available in the toy shops at the time. The clockwork version, with matching articulated coaches and track as shown here, was only available before the war. Also available was an 0-6-2 tank engine in each of the four main-line colours. Just before the war, a 4-6-2 *Duchess of Atholl* and its coaches were advertised but never produced. Clockwork propulsion was not re-introduced after the war.

The next three tracks are from the Trix series. Introduced in 1935, it was destined to be available in this form for about twenty-five years, and the company was to have nearly as many owners. Powered on 14 Volts AC, with automatic reversing, they had the same tendencies as their 'O' gauge 20 Volt contemporaries in that they would reverse just when you did not want them to. The upper train of those shown is the LNER passenger set with the teak-style coaches then in prototype use; below is the LMS goods train. The wagon immediately behind the tank engine is another example of the model manufacturer having an open wagon in his own livery, although these did not exist in reality. Bassett-Lowke had a very similar one in 'O' gauge. The remainder do reflect wagons in use on the real railways. One interesting habit that Trix had was to leave space in the set boxes for the second train when purchased. Both Trix and Hornby used different couplings after the war.

The bottom two tracks contain trains from the Bing range of 1924 to 1926. These were available in clockwork or 4–6 Volt electric, and the range included a 2-4-0 tender locomotive. All the accessories are clip-fitted to the track, including the signals, which were back to front. Even these smaller items followed their larger brethren in having an LNWR flavour, whatever colours they carried.

POWER
HORNBY

13 HORNBY TRAINS

By the late 1920s, and throughout the 1930s, Hornby trains were by far the most popular models in England. A large selection, reasonable prices and distribution in nearly every toy shop were the factors that were mainly responsible for this popularity. To ensure that, once a boy had started with Hornby, he kept to it, the *Meccano Magazine* instituted the Hornby Railway Company, a club for all owners, and emphasized the fact that the Hornby system was so complete. Although not by any means a 'scale' system, the items shown here illustrate that the range was a fair representation.

From top left to bottom right, we start with a signal cabin. This is from the 1920s, and it includes the special feature of an opening roof and back for use with the Hornby Control System. This was a system of points and signals operated from miniature levers housed inside the signal cabin.

The Southern Railway 4-4-0 No. 900 *Eton* is from the famous Schools class, which were the most powerful engines of this wheel arrangement in Europe. Often these models are added to the list of famous Hornby No. 2 Special 4-4-0s, but in fact they were allocated the number 4C for the clockwork type shown, or E420 for the electric version. This locomotive and the Great Western coaches shown with it were introduced in 1937.

The LNER 4-4-4 tank engine is from the mid-1920s and it displays certain similarities to German products, as did others at this time. These particular engines came in many liveries; for instance, there are at least four different LMS types. They were superseded in the early 1930s by the more popular 4-4-2 types. The two coal wagons in this train are in liveries created by Hornby for advertising purposes. The Power Ethyl petrol tank wagon is just one of the many available. At the back is one of the first vans available in the early 1920s.

The Great Western 0-4-0 is a No. 1 type from the 1930s. These tank engines started in the 1920s and lasted until 1966, with many variations. This particular example had the honour of appearing as the star of a television play in 1968. The coal wagon behind completes the set with the two mentioned above, this time bearing the name of the sister product.

L N E R
4472
L M S
6100
3433
5374
112

14 BASSETT-LOWKE

The Bassett-Lowke models shown here span the twenty-five years from 1915 to 1940, and, except for the middle one, they are of local manufacture.

Top picture: This is what must now be the most famous of all steam locomotives. The model is from the 1930s, when the *Flying Scotsman* was a member of the growing family of Pacifics used for working the 10 a.m. express of the same name from King's Cross. It was exhibited at the Wembley Exhibition of 1924, and worked the first regular non-stop run between London and Edinburgh in 1928.

Second picture: The 10 a.m. departure from Euston for Scotland was called the *Royal Scot* from the summer of 1928. To work this train Henry Fowler hurriedly designed and had built a series of 4-6-0s, the first of which was called the *Royal Scot*. The model shown here is from the mid 1930s, and it reflects the contemporary condition of the prototype. In 1933 it was exhibited, with its train, at the Chicago World Fair, and afterwards toured North America.

Third picture: This locomotive is the odd man out for this page because it is another that was produced by Bing on Bassett-Lowke's behalf. Introduced in 1915, it is based on the Great Western Railway 4-4-0 *City of Bath*. Compared with the Great Western model shown in plate 5, it is a scale model which includes the correct number and name combination.

Fourth picture: This locomotive is another of the types which had a long run. It was introduced in 1930 in LMS, LNER and Southern Railway liveries with simplified valve gear. The model shown is de-luxe version.

Fifth picture: Here we have a famous 112 tank engine. Introduced just before World War I, it was produced in 'O' and '1' gauges and was driven by clockwork, electricity or steam, with a multitude of liveries. The permutations appear to be endless, and the model shown here is clockwork 'O' gauge. The number, incidentally, derives from Bassett-Lowke's famous Holborn address.

LNER
UNION PACIFIC
COACH
UNION PACIFIC
M-10000

15 STREAMLINING

During the 1930s speed and streamlining replaced the austerity of the Depression period a few years earlier. The trains shown here represent the toy manufacturers' interpretations of an English steam express and an American diesel electric unit.

The diesel electric is a product of Louis Marx from their American factory, and it shows the experimental streamlined train of the Union Pacific Railroad. The streamlining had been designed after wind-tunnel tests with models, and for lightness-with-strength the complete three-coach unit was built as an aluminium tube, the whole weighing only 85 tons fully loaded. With such a light loading it was possible to carry it on four bogies, which was done by articulation. The connection between each coach, in both the real train and the model, was achieved by a special locking pin. The real train was up-rated to six cars, and broke all railway records in 1934 when it covered the 3,259 miles between Los Angeles and New York in 56 hours 56 minutes.

The silver steam train next to this again comes from Louis Marx, but this time is an English product. It represents the LNER crack express *The Silver Jubilee;* it was also known as the 'Silver Link', this being the name of the locomotive which worked the train. The engine has only four driving wheels, with a weight in the front for balance and adhesion. Both these Marx models have threaded keys, but on different sides.

At the top right of the picture is the Hornby version, which came under their MO range but was primarily intended only to be run as the train shown. The coaches are articulated, but they run on single axles and not bogies.

None of the models shown has reversing gear, presumably because it was unlikely to see the prototype reversing, and it also kept costs down.

The Silver Jubilee was born from the idea of running a train such as the diesel *Flying Hamburger* of Germany. Introduced in September 1935, the Silver Jubilee year of His Majesty King George V, and with its then-novel streamlined shape painted in silver and grey, it caused a sensation. The whole train had been specially designed and painted to match the four special engines allocated to working it on the four-hour service between London and Newcastle at an average speed of 67 mph.

"Princess Elizabeth"
6201
L M S
The HORNBY Clockwork Train
BUILT OF STANDARDISED PARTS
HORNBY TRAIN
BRITISH AND GUARANTEED

16 HOW THEY CAME

This page is devoted to Hornby packing methods, with the one exception of *Impudence* at the top of the page. Packing is, I am afraid, something that the British have never really excelled in, and the sets shown here are typical of what I have seen.

At the top is the *Princess Elizabeth* in its presentation box. Introduced in April 1937, and costing 5 guineas complete, it was the most expensive locomotive ever produced by Hornby. On the lid of the presentation box are inscribed the details of the run made by the real engine in November 1936, when it covered the 400 miles between London and Glasgow at an average speed of 70 mph. On the right is a picture and details of the Hornby model. Unfortunately for later collectors, the wheels, valve gear and parts on the tender were cast in a material which deteriorates even without wear and tear. Providing the extreme comparison on the lid is the first engine in the M series: numbered 2526, which is derived from its period of introduction, it is probably the smallest type produced by Hornby in 'O' gauge.

The LNWR set below this is one of the first productions in the 1920s. The idea of producing trains came from the 'Meccano' construction system, and the locomotive and rolling stock were made so that they could be taken apart and re-assembled, as the instructions on the lid show. This method did not last long, rivets taking over from the nuts and bolts. The locomotive has no prototype markings, but the coaches carry the LNWR crest. The track shown was changed shortly afterwards to the familiar three-sleeper type.

At the bottom is a set from the late 1930s. This type of box was the last, because in the post-war period it was used with detail differences. The train is 20 Volt AC electric and would require a transformer to operate. The power from the transformer was fed to the track via the controller, shown in front of the engine, and the connector, which clip-fits to any straight piece of track. The box lid was always ambitious, but then so were a lot of others. The number used on the locomotive 793 was that of *Sir Ontzlake* of the King Arthur 4-6-0s.

Over the years there were many other manufacturers who achieved various degrees of success—Mettoy and Chad Valley in England and Bub and Kraus on the Continent. It would be impossible to do justice to them all in one volume but we hope to have given some idea of what was available. To those old enough we hope to have brought back memories, and to others perhaps we have whetted the appetite. None of the models were 'scale models' but they were representations. The 0-4-0s from most makers were usually the cheapest while, of course, the better types were more expensive.

There is still quite a lot of material in circulation but, of course, it is becoming scarce as more of it goes into collections. First designed principally as toys the models sometimes look as if they have been played with every day whilst others come as if they were new. Even those items beyond repair are always worth having for spares which are no longer available. Tin-plate trains with body damage can usually be straightened out with small tools and fingers. Paintwork damage is a more debatable question. There are two distinct schools of thought here: one says that no attempt should be made to repaint, whilst the other says that it is acceptable if properly done.

Mechanical repairs can usually be done at home but if in doubt there are one or two places which carry them out. Unfortunately some Hornby locomotives suffer with metal fatigue in their wheels and other castings. There is, I am afraid, no cure except to replace where possible.

More information is something we all require, but there is not much material readily available. Old catalogues, books and magazines, such as *Meccano Magazine* and the *Hornby Book of Trains,* are, of course, ideal but are becoming more rare due to demand. There was a book on collecting published in America but it is long out of print. A couple of English firms have produced catalogues of interest to collectors. Bassett-Lowke Railways of London issued their catalogue, which is interesting for the second-hand items shown and for the reprints from earlier catalogues. The other reprint available is the Meccano products catalogue for 1937, produced by Acorn Models of Swansea. Both these catalogues are essential for collectors.

APPENDIX 1

SCALES AND GAUGES

In the early days there were no accepted standards of work. Henry Greenly issued details of what he thought should be accepted, and gradually, though with one or two exceptions, for there have always been the odd manufacturers whose equipment did not match anyone else's, they came to be accepted by the majority. The generally accepted gauges were:

Gauge 4	3-inch	Gauge 76 mm	
,, 3	2½-inch	,, 64 mm	
,, 2	2-inch	,, 51 mm	
,, 1	1¾-inch	,, 45 mm	10 mm — 1 ft
,, O	1¼-inch	,, 32 mm	7 mm — 1 ft
,, OO	⅝-inch	,, 16·5 mm	4 mm — 1 ft
,, HO	⅝-inch	,, 16·5 mm	3·5 mm — 1 ft

There were differences of detail in scales used in the United States:

Standard gauge 2	2⅛-inch	55 mm	
,, 1	1⅞-inch	48 mm	
,, O	1¼-inch	32 mm	¼-inch scale
,, S	⅞-inch		
,, HO	⅝-inch	16·5 mm	3·5 mm — 1 ft

The gauge is always measured as the distance between the inside of each running rail, and the scale is the measurement to equal 1 ft to match each gauge.

APPENDIX 2

TRADE MARKS

These are always interesting, and some of them can lead to guessing games. Most of the types we have talked about should provide no real difficulty but one or two may not be perfectly clear. These have been kindly redrawn for me by Jim Preston, and are shown below.

Some of the Bing for Bassett-Lowke carries no mark at all but is easily identified. Some manufacturers such as Hornby and Bassett-Lowke had a number of different marks. The Louis Marx sign is the same for both English and American models.

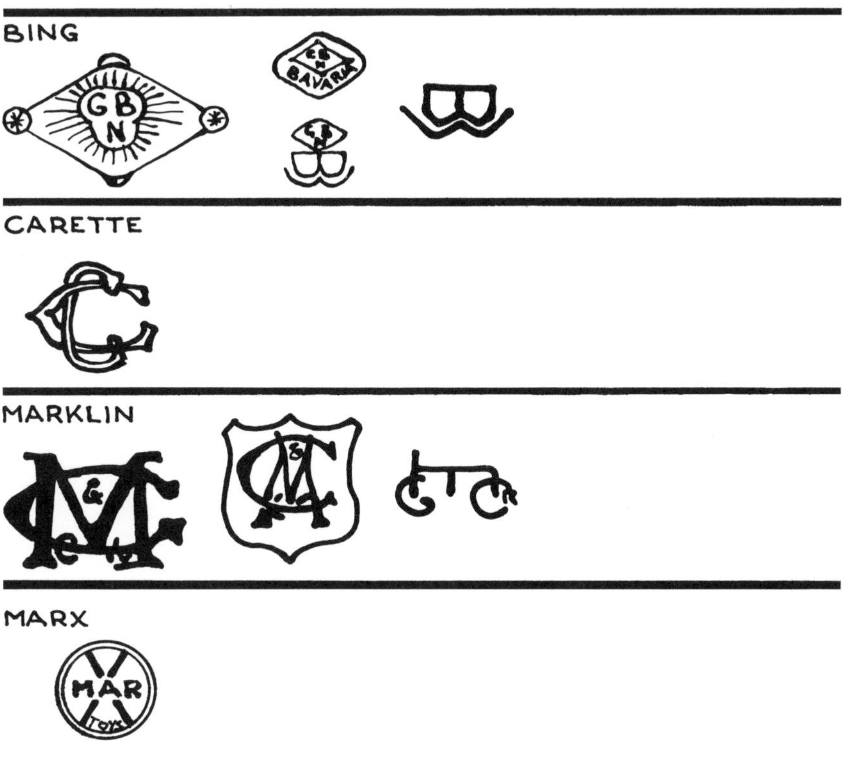

INDEX

Q

R

S

T

V

W

THE TROY MODEL CLUB

In the last few years the amount of interest shown in models of all kinds has grown fantastically. The variety and number produced by manufacturers has barely kept up with the demand. Often they are not so much toys but highly accurate and detailed scale miniatures. Yet the length of time any particular model stays in production is often very limited. Surprisingly, books recording this world boom have been few and far between and have seldom shown models in colour.

The Troy Model Club Series has been launched in order to fill this need. Each volume will be illustrated only in colour and will deal with the development and history of popular ranges of models in Britain, Europe and the U.S.A. Well-known specialists have agreed to write for the series.

We would like everyone interested in models to become a member of the club and to tell us what variety of models they want to see covered in future volumes. There is no age limit. We are catering equally for the under-ten's, the over-ten's, their fathers and their grandfathers.

Our concern has been with manufactured models and those made from plastic kits, because this appears to be where the need for books is greatest. Later, we hope to publish volumes which will include individual models constructed by the knowledgeable enthusiast.

The first four books in the series are:

VETERAN AND VINTAGE CARS Cecil Gibson

COMMERCIAL VEHICLES Cecil Gibson

OLDER LOCOMOTIVES (1900-42) P. G. Gomm

RECENT LOCOMOTIVES (1947-70) P. E. Randall

Many other volumes are in preparation.

The launching of the Troy Model Club will be exciting news for everyone who buys, borrows, studies and collects models, for model engineering clubs, for schools, libraries, toy shops and even manufacturers! For membership of the Club, complete the form on the jacket of this book and send it to:

The Secretary The Troy Model Club 36 Park Street London W 1

OTHER TITLES IN THE SERIES NOW AVAILABLE

RECENT LOCOMOTIVES (1947-70) P. E. Randall
In *Recent Locomotives* Mr Randall shows the fascinating panorama of post-war model railways: the clockwork 'O' gauge 'freelance' tin-plate models, in their gay liveries of red, blue or green; the more realistic diecast 'OO' gauge, modelling such great locomotives as the *Flying Scotsman,* the *Mallard* and the *Britannia;* and the tiny 'N' gauge, whose locomotives can be fitted into a matchbox!
SBN 17 213209 6

VETERAN AND VINTAGE CARS Cecil Gibson
Dr Gibson is a lively and knowledgeable guide to the story of the models of veteran and vintage cars *and* the originals they represent. Beautifully made and painted, and accurate to the last detail, such models have become collectors' items, faithfully mirroring the simple mechanism of the veteran cars, the stateliness of the Edwardians and the tremendous technical advances made during the vintage decade after World War I. The whole history of motoring is here available in miniature in superb colour plates.
SBN 17 213206 1

COMMERCIAL VEHICLES Cecil Gibson
Dr Gibson's lively text outlines the development of the commercial vehicle, from the small, squat shapes early in this century to the sleek vans and vast tankers and carriers of today, and from steam carriage to Routemaster. As can be seen in the plates of this book, some models are small bursts of colour, with delightful decals added to their bright paintwork advertising tea, biscuits, newspapers, petrol and many other proprietary goods.
SBN 17 213207 X

All 210 x 149 mm 64 pp 16 colour plates with 4-colour laminated jacket.

ALSO COMING SHORTLY

RACING AND RECORD CARS Cecil Gibson

Dr Gibson outlines the fascinating development of racing cars, rally cars, sports cars and record-breaking cars, from the 130-hp Fiat that won the 1907 French Grand Prix to Graham Hill's Lotus 49B, and from Sir Henry Segrave's 1929 *Golden Arrow* to Donald Campbell's ill-fated *Bluebird*. The colour plates show that the models, like their full-size counterparts, are brightly painted, carry a suggestion of speed and power, and are often extremely beautiful.

SBN 17 213210 X

MILITARY VEHICLES Jack Wheldon

It would be very hard to find any-one who has not at some time fallen under the spell of military models. In *Military Vehicles* Jack Wheldon describes the growth of mechanized armour from World War I to the present day, and the way its spectacular growth has affected battle strategy. The plates show a fascinating variety of tanks, self-propelled guns, lorries, missile-launchers and amphibious vehicles, and make these miniatures delightfully real to us.

SBN 17 213211 8

TROY MODEL CLUB SERIES · TROY MODEL CLUB SERIES · TROY MODEL CLUB SERIES ·